the
linde werdelin
ski guide

FRANCE

Beautiful
Books

We are both keen freeskiers. Growing up in Denmark, we have been skiing together in the Alps since the age of six. Over the years, we have built our knowledge of the best runs, hotels and restaurants in each resort and have put this guide book together to share our experiences of skiing and the mountain lifestyle with you.

In 2006, we produced the first ski guide book for Switzerland, since then we have expanded the range to include France and Italy. We will be updating and expanding the guide books each year, as we continue to find new gems, to provide you with the first hand information you need to experience superior skiing.

Our passion for skiing was one of the inspirations behind the founding of LINDE WERDELIN in 2002 and we hope that you too will find inspiration through the exploration of the peaks and valleys of the alps; you may even find a hidden gem even we do not know of.

We hope you have excellent skiing conditions and enjoy this season.

OUR COMMANDMENTS

1. Always plan ahead, always place safety first and wear top quality equipment.

2. Remember to wear an avalanche beacon – always – and know how to use it. There is no good reason not to. Also make sure your skiing partner knows how to use it otherwise it's not much help for you.

3. Never ski outside the marked areas without a guide – it is just not worth the risk however harmless it looks. Besides, a good mountain guide makes everything worth skiing better.

4. When you ski with a guide only share the day with another three friends. Too many people slows the day down and limits the guide's ability to guide.

5. Always make sure your skis are properly serviced and waxed with sharp edges (87-88 degrees for steep and hard skiing). Too often people think it is extravagant to spend CHF 50/€ 30 for an overnight service when they wouldn't think twice about spending this on a starter!

6. Make sure you are properly hydrated in the morning and throughout the day. You will feel much fresher and stronger when skiing.

7. Check the weather (eg: barometer trend) in the

morning to avoid any nasty surprises. It will help you plan your day – and decide whether to book for lunch inside or outside.

8. Boots, skis and other equipment in general should be as good as you expect your skiing to be. We have found that skis keep for 100-150 days of skiing or a maximum of 3 years; and boots 150-200 days or 5 years max. It makes a tremendous difference to your enjoyment and safety to have tight fitting boots and skis that match your skills, weight and

CHAMONIX

style—most people underestimate the importance of skis.

9. To master your skiing it's best to divide your time over the season, don't go only once—go for a weekend, a week, a few days or longer if you can! Otherwise you may not get the fantastic days that you will remember.

10. Have fun!

Chamonix (1,035 m) itself is not universally pretty but rather a mix of old world charm, including car-free cobblestone streets, cosy bars and bistros, and horrible concrete towers built in the 1970s.

However, Chamonix has moved upmarket over the last decade, a bit like Val d'Isère though less organised.

For Alpine beauty go deeper into the valley and stay in Le Praz, Le Lavancher, Argentière or Les Bois. All around you is a panorama of steep cliffs and massive seas of glacial seracs, all lorded over by Mont Blanc (4,808 m), as well as the spectacular Aiguille du Midi and the Grands Montets.

These features give Chamonix the wild beauty that has attracted skiers and climbers the world over for generations. Chamonix has something for everyone, it is welcoming and unpretentious and a bit like a second home from home.

This is one area we have skied the most through the years – and somehow we always return for more.

SURROUNDINGS

Aiguille du Midi (3,842 m)

The Aiguille du Midi cable car is a stupendous achievement in engineering, but the surrounding terrain is even more spectacular.

La Vallée Blanche is the classic run from the top over the Mer de Glace, a 24 km descent. It is easy enough for intermediates with the help of a guide, but can also be recommended for experts as a nature experience. It's the longest run in the world, taking skiers an amazing 2,800 m vertical back to Chamonix and passes over and through an icy, crevasse-filled landscape that cannot be equalled in beauty anywhere in Europe. The base station of the cable car was rebuilt last

year and is set to finish this season with new hotels, shops and restaurants. Experts will prefer such alternatives as L'Envers du Plan or the Glacier Rond. You can also ski to the Italian side for a good technical descent to the Courmayeur Valley. At the mid station the Pavillon Restaurant is an ideal stop to test the Italian cuisine before returning to France with the Helbronner cable car.

While there are no official seasonal opening times for the Aiguille du Midi, you should be sure to check snow conditions and the weather forecast before heading out and it is strongly recommended you take a mountain guide with you. (see Guides)

Brévent (2,525 m) and La Flégère (2,385 m)

Slightly to the south of Chamonix, and connected by the Brévent cable car to the town, the Brévent ski area has some rather extreme couloirs that descend all the way back to town, but most skiers will remain on the upper slopes, which link up with the La Flégère area outside town. These mountains face south and are particularly recommended on sunny, powdery mornings during January when it is too cold elsewhere.

In March and April, the corn snow sparkles and beckons and you can shift into fifth gear and fly, for the crowds are somewhere else. By 11:30, the snow is too soft and it is time to move on. Almost all visitors to these areas download on the cable cars, so don't

get caught here late in the day without a newspaper to keep you happy. Or take the new high speed gondola from Plan Praz to Chamonix.

From the top of Brévent you can go touring to Servoz through a valley which is a conservation area. Other touring routes starting in Brévent/La Flégère take you through spectacular valleys and ridges end in France or Switzerland. Le Brévent ski area is open from December to April. La Flégère ski area is open from December to May.

Les Grands Montets (3,275 m)

Situated in Argentière (1,252 m) and accessed with the Lognan cable car, the Grands Montets is the most exciting mountain in the Chamonix Valley. The morning after a heavy snowfall, the unloading area of the uppermost cable car resembles a Friday evening rush out of London, but it is all worthwhile to get first tracks on one of the world's best mountains.

There are stupendous off-piste tours among the seracs of the glacier off the back side and classic off-piste tours such as Pas de Chèvre and Rectiligne. One of our favourite off-piste routes is to ski the trees in powder down to the village of Le Lavancher. Descents from the top are about 2,000 m vertical. Les Grands Montets is open from December (sometimes earlier if snow conditions allow for it) to May.

MOUNTAINS

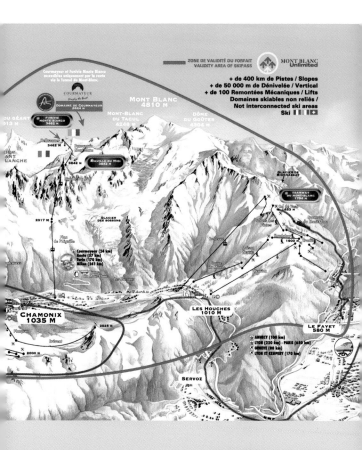

MOUNTAIN GUIDES

Franck Moscatello at Guides des Baronnies

Our good friend Franck has been skiing with Jorn since the early 1990s and knows the Chamonix valley better than anyone else. Guides des Baronnies epitomises the true spirit of skiing, offering all kinds of ski tours, heli-ski and lessons around Chamonix.

+33 (0)608 56 95 58   www.guidesdesbaronnies.com

Fabrice Biraghi

An independant high mountain guide who has been skiing in Chamonix for over 20 years. Fabrice "Bibi" is the one to see for extreme off-piste skiing.

+33 (0)6 86 97 14 56   www.skicoaches-mountainguides.com

HELI-SKI

Although heli-skiing is illegal in France, it is easy to get across the border to Italy or Switzerland.

Heliski Valgrisenche

In Italy is a great place for heli-skiing. It is one heli-ski plus a small albergo at the end of the road – with excellent espresso. Some years back we had four lifts before 2:00 pm and a long leisurely lunch afterwards with local grappa to finish off – beautiful.

When booking ask for Danilo Garin.

+39 3 496 649 763   www.heliskivalgrisenche.it

Big Dreams

Is run by Swede "Jossi" Lindblom. They arrange tours
and weeks in Chamonix, La Grave and heli-ski in
Riksgränsen in May – phenomenal ! If you should go
to Riksgräsen stay at the hotel Metropol which might
be the culinary highlight north of the arctic circle.

+33 (0)4 50 54 13 90   www.bigdreams.se

Chamonix Aventures

Offer drops in Monte Rosa, Val Veny and Valais or
for something different they organise trips to Russia,
Turkey, Iceland, Bulgaria and Chile.

+33 (0)9 77 76 13 62   www.chamonix-aventure.com

Elemental Adventure

We also recommend James Morland at Elemental
Adventure if you prefer a Chamonix-based operation.
They will look after you like friends. They also organise
trips worldwide.

+44 (0) 207 836 3547 / +33 (0)6 20 43 65 88
www.eaheliskiing.com/europe-heli-skiing/chamonix-heliski

RESTAURANTS

MOUNTAIN RESTAURANTS
Unfortunately, Chamonix doesn't offer a lot of good mountain restaurants although it is slowly improving.

Chalet-Refuge de Lognan
At Les Grands Montets is definitely one of the best. Overlooking the Argentière glacier it has wonderful French country cuisine, fantastic home-made tarts and always a good atmosphere. It is very popular so book in advance. They also have a few rooms you can stay in. To get there keep right of the glacier when skiing under the La Herse lift.
+33 (0)4 50 54 10 21

Auberge des 3 Ours
In Vallorcine has a mountain farm ambience, great grills and an authentic feel.
Le Plan Droit, 74660 Vallorcine   +33 (0)4 54 63 06

Crémerie du Glacier
In the forest at the bottom of the slope of the Grands Montets at the foot of the Lognan cable car. Traditional cosy wood chalet, good for local cheese dishes and worth discovering.
330, route des Rives, 74400   +33 (0)4 50 55 90 10

Les Vieilles Luges
Hidden in the forest, between the two ski lifts, close to the foot of Les Houches ski slopes, accessible by ski,

but also by a 20 minute walk from Maisonneuve car park. The restaurant is a 250-year-old alpine farm and can be busy both during the day and in the evenings; therefore it is advisable to book ahead.
+33 (0)6 84 42 37 00

L'Arrêt Bougnette
At the bottom of the Vallorcine side to the right of the train station, serves typical and local dishes "Le Bertoud".
Plan de L'envers, 74660 Valloricine   +33 (0)4 50 54 63 04

RESTAURANTS IN TOWN

Albert 1er–Part of « Le Hameau Albert 1er »

The Hameau Albert 1er's signature restaurant where Michelin starred chefs Pierre Maillet and Pierre Carrier create seasonal gastronomic menus. They stock an extensive wine cellar of almost 19,000 bottles carefully looked after by head sommelier, Christian Martray.

38, route du Bouchet, 74400   +33 (0)4 50 53 05 09

Maison Carrier–Part of « Le Hameau Albert 1er »

The second restaurant in the Hameau Albert 1er is La Ferme. One of the best in town (and the Alps) serving traditional local specialities and more. Dine by the fire in traditional Savoyard farmhouse style or on the sunny terrace facing Mont Blanc.

38, route du Bouchet, 74400   +33 (0)4 50 53 05 09

L'Impossible

An 18th century barn that has been converted into a fine dining restaurant by extreme skier Sylvain Saudan. The specialty is meat cooked on a chimney fire.

9, chemin du Cry, 74400   +33 (0)4 50 53 20 36

Le Bistrot Chamonix

At the Hotel Morgane was recently refurbished. Michelin starred chef Mickey is one of the best chefs in France. Excellent service.

151, avenue de l'Aiguille du Midi, 74400   +33 (0)4 50 53 57 64

Casa Valerio

If you get tired of French cuisine come here for excellent wood fired pizza (more than 50 types) and pasta. Eating at the bar is also recommended.

Popular with locals and open all afternoon.

Next door is the new Italian Osteria, The Dolce Vista.

88, rue Lyret, 74400   +33 (0)4 50 55 93 40

Eden

At Les Praz is a well kept secret. Well priced and sophisticated French menu. Ideal for pre-dinner drinks in front of the fireplace and to watch the sunset.

35, route des Gaudenays, 74400   +33 (0)4 50 53 18 43

L'Atmosphère

A local favourite with good views and an even better selection of Savoie wines (over 300) and gastronomic cuisine. Cosy chalet-style décor with a covered terrace overlooking the Arve river. Has a Michelin star and booking is advised.

123, place Balmat, 74400   +33 (0)4 50 55 97 97

La Cabane des Praz

A beautifully restored log cabin with a contemporary interior located in the Hotel Labrador in front of the Chamonix Golf course, La Cabane des Praz is a wonderful combination of traditional alpine living and modern chic. This combination is carried over into the restaurant's menu, which presents a choice of traditional food with a modern twist; their 'hot stone' dishes are particularly recommended, especially if you are in a group.

27, route du Golf, 74400   +33 (0)4 50 53 23 27

APRÈS-SKI

Quartz bar
The latest addition to the «Hameau Albert 1er», offering a selection of teas and homemade pastries in the afternoons and becoming an animated wine bar at night, with live Jazz and Lounge music, provided by the inspirational musician, Samir Hodzik.
A chic and comfortable bar, based entirely on themes of crystal and ice.

38, route du Bouchet, 74400   +33 (0)4 50 53 05 09

Atelier Café
Open until 7 pm and has a good selection of wines by the glass. With an outside terrace close to the river it has a calm and soothing atmosphere.

812, quai de l'Arve 74400   +33 (0)4 50 53 32 36

MBC Micro Brasserie Chamonix
A Canadian pub with good live music and local beers which you can see being brewed. Just outside Chamonix on the road to Argentière near the sports centre.

350, rue de bouchet, 74400   +33 (0)4 50 53 61 59

Chambre Neuf
An ideal place to start the night. A favourite meeting place for locals and visitors, it has a fun and busy vibe.

272, av. Michel Croz, 74400   +33 (0)4 50 55 89 81

L'Elévation 1904
A café bar that challenges Chambre Neuf for the premier après-ski spot.

259, av. Michel Croz, 74400 +33 (0)4 50 53 00 52

Le Lapin Agile
A great wine bar with a selection from around the world. Also good for light Italian meals.

11, rue Whymper, 74400 +33 (0)4 50 53 33 25

Le Privelege
Lounge bar open from 4:00 pm to 2:00 am for the more discerning clientele.

Rue des Moulins, 74400 +33 (0)6 33 76 86 00

The Clubhouse
Serves the best cocktails and is a great place for a relaxing drink by candlelight.

This members-only bar, restaurant and boutique hotel is run by the same owners as Milk & Honey in London and New York. Non-members can make dinner reservations by calling first.

74, promenade des Sonnailles, 74400 +33 (0)4 50 90 96 56

La Terrasse
One of the largest and busiest bars in Chamonix provides a friendly, professional service.
Often live music.

43, place Balmat, 74400 +33 (0)4 50 53 09 95

HOTELS

Hotel Hameau Albert 1er – Part of « Le Hameau Albert 1er »

The best hotel in Chamonix. This 100-year-old chalet-style hotel is the epitome of luxury and character, developed over five generations of hoteliers. Facilities include an indoor/outdoor swimming pool, spa, jacuzzi, steam room, sauna and fitness room, all located in a true-to-life hamlet only a 5-minute walk from Chamonix centre.

38, route du Bouchet, 74400

+33 (0)4 50 53 05 09   www.hameaualbert.fr

La Ferme – Part of « Le Hameau Albert 1er »

Also part of Le Hameau and known as the 'Farmhouse'. Offering 12 chic and authentic rooms, with all contemporary amenities.

38, route du Bouchet, 74400

+33 (0)4 50 53 05 09   www.hameaualbert.fr

Jeu de Paume

Halfway towards Argentière at Le Lavancher. A good place to stay with a group of friends and not have to venture into town too often.

It has a classic atmosphere with a beautiful see-through fireplace and is quite reasonable.

With a little updating this could be a top notch Alpine hotel.

705, route du Chapeau, 74400, Le Lavancher

+33 (0)4 50 54 03 76   www.jeudepaumechamonix.com

Eden

A nice basic option with a friendly and welcoming atmosphere. It is located near Les Praz and has a certain Scandinavian style to it; the couple who owns it are from Sweden.

35, route des Gaudenays, 74400 Les Praz

+33 (0)4 50 53 18 43   www.hoteleden-chamonix.com

Auberge du Bois Prin

Ideal for peace and quiet on the Moussoux heights of the south side. Dine at the restaurant for a panoramic view of Mont Blanc.

69, chemin de l'hermine, Les Moussoux, 74400

+33 (0)4 50 53 33 51   www.boisprin.com

La Chapelle d'Elisa

A great alternative if you want to get out of the centre of town. A converted chapel, it is the smallest hotel in Les Grands Montets (and maybe even the smallest in all of the Alps). Ski-in ski-out, but for the experienced skier only.

394, chemin de la Rosière, 74400 Argentière
+33 (0)4 50 54 00 17

THINGS TO DO

As one of the most popular ski destinations in Europe, Chamonix provides a wealth of winter entertainment and events; ranging from concert festivals to international ski championships, Chamonix never ceases to entertain.
Contact the Tourist Board Office in Chamonix for the annual itinerary (see Useful Contacts).

Ski touring

Discover Ski Touring in the Chamonix Valley. Take the lift system and it's an hour's walk to access fantastic off-piste skiing and virgin powder. Look out for wild animals on the way.

The service of a guide will guarantee the best choice for the day and be sure to find the right way back to the valley! Ask Franck Moscatello (see Guides).

Dog sledding

An alternative way to see the region.
Husky Dalen provides both half-day and full-day courses.
+33 (0)4 50 47 77 24   www.huskydalen.com

Paragliding

Book at Chamonix-Parapente for tandem flights across Les Grands Montets, Aiguille du Midi or Brévent.
Ask for Fred, Herve or Christophe.
+33 (0)6 61 84 61 50   www.chamonix-parapente.fr

Guided Heritage Visits

Retracing the rich history and architecture of Chamonix, discover the history of this iconic town through the rich architecture of its buildings.
+33 (0)4 50 53 00 24

Alpine Museum

Housed in the old 'Chamonix Palace', the museum documents the history of Chamonix, from the arrival of the first tourists through to its position as an international destination for winter sports.
+33 (0)4 50 53 25 93

Food market

A traditional food market is held every Saturday morning from 8:00am to 12:00pm. The best you can get in local cheeses, meats, oysters, breads, fruit, vegetables and other delicacies.

SPAS AND RELAXATION

Bachal

Attached to the Hameau Albert 1er, Bachal offers a variety of treatments to revive the body and spirit after a long day on the mountain slopes.

38, route du Bouchet, 74400   +33 (0)4 50 53 05 09

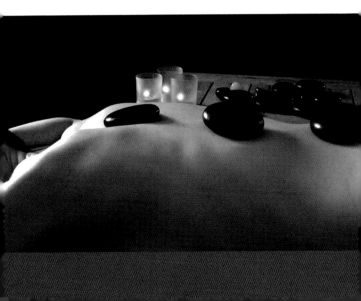

TRAVEL

Geneva, Turin and Lyon airports serve Chamonix, all three offer a variety of public transport and private hire services to Chamonix. But it is recommended to hire a car when skiing in Chamonix.

SAT

SAT operates out of Geneva and provides a regular shuttle service between the airport and Chamonix with stops at Chamonix, Les Houches and Le Fayet.

+33 (0)4 50 53 01 15   www.sat-montblanc.com

Savda

This public transport line provides services that run between Turin airport and Chamonix train station.

+39 (0)165 26 20 27   www.savda.it

Lyon by Train

There is a direct and regular line between Lyon and Chamonix train station. The TGV website also provides booking and travel information if you are travelling by train from further afield.

www.tgv.com

PRIVATE TRANSFERS

Mountain Drop Offs

Operating between Geneva airport and the Chamonix airport, Mountain Drop Offs offers both 'shared' and 'private' options.

+33 (0)4 50 47 17 73   www.mountaindropoffs.com

Chamonix Mont Blanc Helicopter

Offering a huge variety of destinations and travel options, why not avoid the seasonal traffic altogether.

+33 (0)4 50 54 13 82   www.chamonix-helico.fr

Taxis

There are a number of taxi companies that service the Chamonix region, the Chamonix tourist board or your hotel are the best people to contact for further information (for Chamonix tourist board, see Useful Contacts).

USEFUL CONTACTS

Chamonix Tourist Board
+33 (0)4 50 53 00 24
www.chamonix.com

Walking and Mountaineering Office of Chamonix
Weather information and conditions.
+33 (0)4 50 53 22 08
www.ohm-chamonix.com
www.chamonix-meteo.com

La Compagnie du Mont-Blanc
Information on ski lift accessibility and timetables.
+33 (0)4 50 53 22 75
www.compagniedumontblanc.fr

EMERGENCY NUMBERS
P.G.H.M. *Mountain rescue*   +33 (0)4 50 53 16 89

Ambulances   +33 (0)4 50 53 46 20

Hospital Centre   +33 (0)4 50 53 84 00

MEGÈVE

If you are skiing in the Chamonix region for three days or longer, you can purchase a Skipass Mont-Blanc, which includes the resorts of Megève (1,100 m) and Les Contamines as well as Saint-Gervais, Courmayeur and a handful of other resorts in the area. Of course, you will need much more than three days to enjoy such a large expanse of terrain.

Megève is by far the most up-market of the group and stands out as the resort whose atmosphere is as different from Chamonix as night and day. People strolling the streets may or may not be skiers, but they are more likely to be wearing jewellery than climbing equipment.

SURROUNDINGS

The Megève ski area is better suited for beginner and intermediate skiers but, at the same time, is exactly the sort of resort where one can sometimes find some excellent powder that goes untracked for days because the area does not attract a large number of off-piste skiers.

The lift system connects with the villages of La Giettaz, Le Christomet, Combloux, and St. Nicolas de Veroce, as well as St. Gervais. You can also ski off-piste down to Les Contamines. Megève's own ski area is made up of three separate sectors - Le Jaillet, Mont d'Arbois, and Rochebrune. The winter season lasts from early December to early April.

Le Jaillet

Is away from the centre of town so often has fewer skiers, making it a good choice. There are a few nice off-piste descents here, which are usually not as risky as some of the off-piste terrain on Mont d'Arbois. Some of the best views of Mt. Blanc can be enjoyed from here.

Mont d'Arbois

The lower slopes of this area are comprised of a lot of broad highways suitable for beginners and intermediates but, as it is the largest of the ski areas, it also has quite a few off-piste possibilities.

Mont Joly

Among the fare offered here is Mt. Joly, where the lift reaches 2,353 m, the highest point in the Megève lift system. With a stiff sustained slope of 30° to 35°, Mt. Joly also has some of the best but most dangerous off-piste skiing in Megève. A traverse away from town brings skiers to various funnel-shaped ravines that go down to the buffalo farm, « La ferme des bisons » (domaine de la Stassaz), an idéal place to stop off for some lunch.

These ravines can be brilliant if the conditions are right, but these gullies can also be a graveyard on avalanche prone days and it is imperative you take a guide.

Alternatively, there are also some south-facing off-piste routes from Mt. Joly to Les Contamines, which are not as steep. You can also often find some untracked snow between the pistes from Mt. Joux down toward Les Communailles, from the Épaule peak to the bottom of the Croix du Christ lift, and from the Princesse lift to the middle station.

Rocherbrune

The actual Rocherbrune lift only goes up to 1,754 m, but this area also includes the Cote 2,000 at the end of the valley, where the terrain is more challenging both on and off the piste.

Megève and Rocherbrune especially also provide excellent opportunities for tree skiing which provides a good alternative should the weather turn against you, or you just want a chance to play around. Within the woods at Rocherbrune, there is a clearing where a lot of fun can be had sliding around the natural bumps.

MOUNTAINS

MOUNTAIN GUIDES

Bruno Beauvais

A great friend of ours who knows the Megève slopes well. Bruno can cater to all levels of experience, but loves safari skiing and can help you discover the hidden gems of the area not visible on the maps.

He also has something of a passion for the local architecture and history and is as knowledgeable as anyone you might find at the tourist office.

+33 (0)6 80 42 65 92

Megève Guides

These regional experts will be able to help you make the most of your time at Megève, with a wealth of knowledge on offer, they are a one stop shop.

+33 (0)4 50 21 55 11   www.guides-megeve.com

EQUIPMENT

Ski Gatch

Located in the heart of the town, this family run shop is a great place to drop by for equipment and some local information.

473, rue Charles Feige, 74120   +33 (0)4 50 21 24 59

THINGS TO DO

With the towns rustic charm, Megève is known almost as much for its history as for skiing. There is a regular rotating calendar of events put on along with regular tours of the old town organised by the Tourist Board and local authority. Contact the Megève Tourist Board for a complete list of events (see Useful Contacts).

Guides Megève

An established company in the area, Guides Megève offer expertise in a variety of outdoor activities, from ice climbing to paragliding.

+33 (0)4 50 21 55 11   www.guides-megeve.com

Dog Sledding - Mont du Villard Nord

Tour the area in the company of 'man's best friend' with this family owned company. Various tariffs and programmes are available.

+33 (0)4 50 21 37 03   www.montduvillardnord.com

Aerocime

Get a new perspective of Megève with these airplane tours of the area and Mont Blanc itself.

+33 (0)4 50 21 03 21   www.aerocime.com

SPAS AND RELAXATION

Les Fermes de Marie

Treat yourself at the spa at Les Fermes de Marie, the best spa in Megève and one of the best in the world.

+33 (0)4 50 93 03 10   Chemin de Riante Colline, 74120

TRAVEL

The closest airports to Megève are Geneva and Lyon (see map page 40). The most convenient way to travel from the airports to Megève is by taxi or private hire; while it is possible to use public transport, the routes are indirect.

Les Transports du Mont-Blanc

Serving not only Lyons and Geneva, but also other destinations, Transports du Mont Blanc provide a 24 hour service; prices, which can be found on their website, are all inclusive.

+33 (0)6 84 71 02 07   www.ltmb.fr

Mont-Blanc Limousines

Offering a full range of services - from shuttle service, private driver, car rental – Mont-Blanc Limousines is sure to be able to cater for your needs.

+33 (0)4 50 90 84 66   www.montblanclimousines.com

Taxis

The Megève area is served by numerous taxi companies, check the Tourist Board website for details (see Useful Contacts).

USEFUL CONTACTS

Megeve Tourist Board
Also responsible for the ski lift system.
+33 (0)4 50 21 27 28
www.megeve.com

For weather information see Chamonix useful contacts
(p. 43).

EMERGENCY NUMBERS
Ambulance   +33 (0)4 50 93 06 78

Hospital   + 33 (0)4 50 47 30 30

Mountain Rescue   +33 (0)4 50 91 28 10

LES CONTAMINES

Les Contamines (1,160 m) is much smaller than Megève and less well known but maintains its authenticity and charm.

Here one can enjoy stunning views of the Mont Blanc Massif, but the village is in a steep valley and does not get as much sun as Megève.

SURROUNDINGS

There are a lot of off-piste possibilities, especially suited for skiers who wish to try their hand away from the marked trails for the first time.

Much of the terrain is relatively gentle, and the wide, open spaces that exist on the upper slopes above the tree line are ideal for those dabbling into the freeride world for the first time. Freeride experts can ski down towards the buffalo farm toward Megève. The route from this side of the mountain is more difficult and at least as avalanche prone as from the Mt. Joly lift, so don't do this without a guide. Almost all the skiing is above the tree line, making the mountain ill-suited for skiing in poor visibility. The slopes are open to skiers from mid-December to early April.

MOUNTAINS

MOUNTAIN GUIDES
Contamines Guides

Local knowledge and seasoned experience make the Contamines guides a fantastic resource in the planning of a great break.

+33 (0)4 50 47 10 08   www.guides-contamines.com

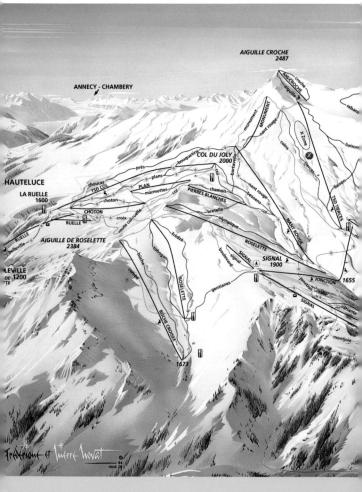

AIGUILLE CROCHE
2487

ANNECY - CHAMBERY

COL DU JOLY
2000

HAUTELUCE

LA RUELLE
1600

PLAN

PIERRES BLANCHES

AIGUILLE DE ROSELETTE
2384

ROSELETTE

SIGNAL
1900

1655

1673

montjoie

RESTAURANTS

MOUNTAIN RESTAURANTS
Auberge de Colombaz
Local recipes with a panoramic terrace with views of Mont Blanc. Arrive by ski taxi and a toboggan descent after dinner; three kilometres from the Naptieu hamlet in the direction of Mont Joly.

+33 (0)4 50 47 01 50

La Roselette
Just off from the lift of the same name, this warm and cosy mountain restaurant is run by the very friendly Cathy and Jean-Pierre Curdel.

At a height of 1871 m the restaurant has fantastic panoramic views to complement the good food and service.

Ld les Chalets la Roselette, 74170   +33 (0)4 50 47 13 31

Ferme de la Ruelle
An old mountain chalet with a south facing terrace, this animated restaurant serves hearty mountain food along with Savoyard specialities under the direction of Cyril the head chef.

604, route des Moranches, 74170   +33 (0)4 79 38 88 30

RESTAURANTS IN TOWN
L'ô à la Bouche

Has two restaurants, dine in L'ô for gastro meals or Marmott's for regional specialites. L'ô is the more refined of the two offering a soothing atmosphere and carefully prepared dishes by chef Fabrice Boidard, the restaurant also acts as a gallery space for local artist Olivier Lehmann. Marmott's is more family friendly in style and is the place to go if you are in a group; they specialise in grilled meats and fondue.

510, route de Notre-Dame de la Gorge, 74170
+33 (0)4 50 47 81 67

L'op Traken

Run by the Lafenchere family, this friendly restaurant at the heart of the village specialise in regional dishes. We particularly recommend the reblochon fondue and their vin chaud.

387, route de Notre-Dame de la Gorge, 74170
+33 (0)4 50 47 03 93

APRÈS-SKI

Ty Breiz

Crêperie that turns into a lively bar.

650, route de Notre-Dame de la Gorge, 74170
+33 (0)4 50 47 18 32

TRAVEL

*As with Chamonix and Megève, Les Contamines has
Lyon and Geneva as its closest major airports (see map
page 40).*

Public Transport
The least expensive option to travel to Les Contamines
is by a direct coach from Geneva airport.
+33 (0)4 50 78 05 33   www.sat-montblanc.com

TAXIS
*If arriving direct from Lyons the best choice is by taxi,
Les Contamines only has one taxi company, therefore
it may be useful to call your hotel or the local Tourist
Board if they cannot meet your requirements.*

Taxi Besson
Les Contamines' local family run taxi service, providing
services to airports and rail stations; there is no
charge for reservation.
+33 (0)4 50 93 61 47

USEFUL CONTACTS

Les Contamines Tourist Board
+33 (0)4 50 47 01 58
www.lescontamines.com

Mountain Guide Office
+33 (0)4 50 47 10 08
www.guides-contamines.com

EMERGENCY NUMBERS
Medical Centre   +33 (0)4 50 47 03 82

NICE SPOT

NOTRE-DAME DE-BELLECOMBE
Is a fifteen minute drive from Megève and is one of our favourite hidden spots after a big snowfall and when the other resorts are closed.

You will find no-one off-piste except for the local mountain guide, Jojo, and his clients.
+33 (0)6 80 68 68 10

Ferme de Victorine
If you visit here be sure to dine at Ferme de Victorine, a cosy family farm restaurant where you can see cows through the windows. It's one of the best restaurants of the region.
+33 (0)4 79 31 63 46

COURCHEVEL

Courchevel (1,850 m) is the place to stay in Les Trois Vallées. It is as chic as Paris «its 21st arrondissement». Courchevel is the only French resort that can compete in style, extravagence and luxury with the top Swiss resorts. It may lack in history and mountain ambiance but it makes up for it in fun, food and nightlife. But make no mistake it has some fantastic skiing too.

Courchevel's slopes are mostly north-facing and hold the snow better than Méribel late in the season. It has quite a few black runs that are good fun for mogul fans including Suisses, Jockeys and Jean Blanc, as well as the classic Grand Couloir and the tree-skiing on the lower sections which gives it versatility.

In the Méribel region, the east-west orientation of the slopes is well suited to spring conditions, allowing you to ski the eastern faces like Roc de Fer, Roc des Trois Marches and Mt. de la Challe in the morning and the west facing slopes of Saulire and Mont du Vallon in the afternoon.

Val Thorens is also very snow secure with its high altitude (3,200 m) and lots of north-facing slopes, but the upper lifts are very susceptible to wind and are often closed and there is no skiing below the tree line.

The winter season lasts for four months in Courchevel, from early December until early April.

SURROUNDINGS

Saulire (2,738 m)

If you like moguls, you will certainly enjoy the steep Grand Couloir directly under the Saulire cable car. There are many chutes between the rocks that all join the Grand Couloir further down. The Emile Allais Couloir is one of the most difficult in this area. One can also access the Couloir Tremplin to Méribel from Saulire.

La Tania and Le Praz

There are some black runs and tree-skiing possibilities from atop the Col de la Loz to the villages of La Tania and Le Praz. You can find some good off-piste slopes in the right conditions under the Dou des Lanches

lift. In bad weather, this area can be the best place to be in the entire system, most of which is above the tree line.

Creux Noirs (2,705 m)

From the top of the Creux Noirs ski lift, hike a little past the last tracks to find some virgin lines here after a snowfall.

Vallée des Avals

You will need skins and sweat to earn your turns here, but it could be worthwhile if you truly cherish the powder and it hasn't snowed in a few days.

The relative isolation means you will have to take both Les Trois Vallées and the Signal lifts to reach the heart of Vallée des Avals.

VAL THORENS

Cime de Caron

Reached via one of the largest cable cars in the world. This is the highest sector of Les Trois Vallées and a good place to go right after a snowfall.

St. Pères Couloirs

These couloirs from the Aiguille de Péclet are reachable with a traverse and hike from the Col chairlift across the Glacier de Chavière in. This is our personal favourite in Les Trois Vallées.

North Face

Even more challenging than the St. Pères Couloirs
is the North Face. Higher up the Aiguille de Péclet,
this descent begins with a 50 degree slope where
a misplaced edge can be fatal. This is one of those
descents that you want a guide for and you want him
to have rope with him!

MÉRIBEL

Gébroulaz Glacier

From atop the Col lift you can ski a long, beautiful
descent down to Méribel. This should be done with
a guide.

MOUNTAINS

MOUNTAIN GUIDES
Courchevel-Méribel employ well trained experts.
Courchevel   +33 (0)4 79 01 03 66
Méribel   +33 (0)4 79 00 30 38
www.guides-courchevel-meribel.com

HELI-SKI
Heliski Greenland
Marc Lazzaroni is an experienced mountain guide born and bred in Courchevel.
He skies over 200 days a year and has skied all over the world from Alaska to Tibet and South America to New Zealand. He also operates heli-ski in Greenland where you will be ensured an unexpected and memorable experience.
+33 (0)6 09 41 65 21   www.heliskigreenland.com

EQUIPMENT
Surefoot
A modern clinic for your feet/boots. They make your feet feel like they are directly connected to the edge of your skis. They also have a shop in Val d'Isère.
Le Chamois, rue Park City, 73120   +33 (0)4 79 23 47 46

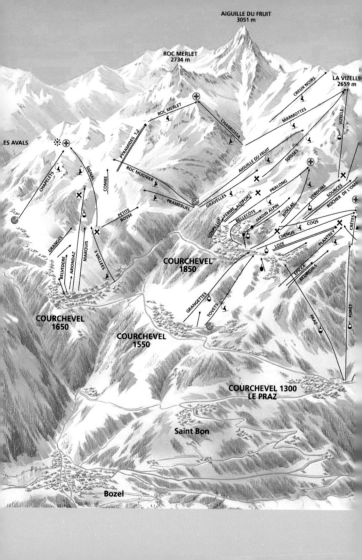

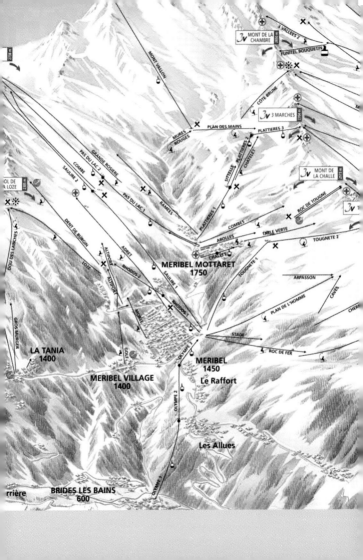

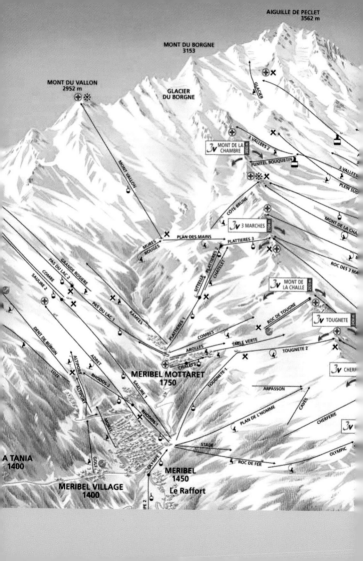

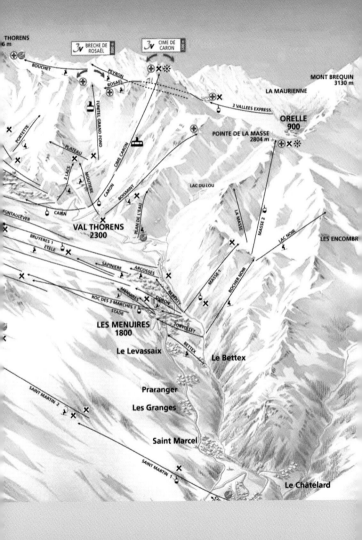

RESTAURANTS

MOUNTAIN RESTAURANTS

Le Cap Horn

The best place at altitude just above the Altiport. A great nautical theme. Good food, an impressive wine list, good cigars and pleasantly popular with a large south-facing terrace.

Courchevel 1850, 73120   +33 (0)4 79 08 33 10

La Bergerie

Converted from an authentic sheephold it has a wonderful slope side terrace and does great burgers. Good atmosphere.

Route de Nogentil, 73120   +33 (0)4 79 08 24 70

La Soucoupe

At the top of the Loze lift.
It serves fantastic grilled meats sometimes barbequed at the fireplace. While they also serve standard steak and fish dishes it is worth trying their specialities such as foie gras pan-fried with onion compote. You must book ahead.

Arrivée téléski de la Loze, 73120   +33 (0)4 79 08 21 34

RESTAURANTS IN TOWN

La Bouitte

Lives up to its Michelin star. If you don't mind missing a few hours of skiing to enjoy a long lunch, cruise down to picturesque St. Marcel to dine here.

Hotel Restaurant La Bouitte, Hameau de Saint Marcel,
73440 Saint Martin de Belleville   +33 (0)4 79 08 96 77

Chabichou

A two star Michelin restaurant. Alpine style with fully modernised interior. International and original cuisine by Michael Rochedy.

Rue des Chenus, Courchevel 1850, 73121
+33 (0)4 79 08 00 55

Bateau Ivre

On the top floor of the Pomme de Pin hotel. Cuisine by Michelin chef Jean Pierre Jacob.

La Pomme de Pin, BP 15, 73121   + 33 (0)4 79 00 11 71

Pierre Gagnaire pour Les Airelles

Renowned chef Pierre Gagnaire creates refined flavours in a setting designed in homage to Sissi the Princess of Bavaria.

Le Jardin Alpin, 73120   +33 (0)4 79 00 38 38

La Saulire

At the centre of the resort facing the clock. Dine on the terrace or in the warm chalet atmosphere. Top notch food from Savoie classics and traditional French to contemporary cuisine. Bookings advised.

Place du Rocher, centre station, 73120   +33 (0)4 79 08 07 52

La Cendrée

Traditional woodfired pizzas and hand-made manicotti and cannelloni single La Cendrée out from the crowd; the extensive selection of Italian wines and champagne and fresh peach juice Bellinis underline that Italian cooking can hold its own even in France.

Le Maroly, 73120   +33 (0)4 79 08 29 38

APRÈS-SKI

La Via Ferrata

A new Italian restaurant in a relaxed atmosphere. There is also a lively bar and it may be a little less full than Le Mangoin.

La Porte de Courchevel, 73120   +33 (0)4 79 08 02 07

La Mangeoire

A local classic that can get very busy, but well worth a visit for the cocktails and the music events, at the piano bar, every evening.

Rue Park City, 73120   +33 (0)4 79 01 05 37

Zinc Bar

Opulent surroundings await at the bar of the Hotel Saint Joseph; for those seeking a quieter night away from the crowds.

Rue Park City, 73120   +33 (0)4 79 08 16 16

La Grange

One of the two most popular clubs in Courchevel 1,850 m, its rustic exterior hides the modern luxury that lies within.

Rue Park City, 73120   +33 (0)4 79 08 14 61

Les Caves de Courchevel

The second of Courchevel's club venues, at Les Caves you will see truly large bottles of champagne being handed around.

Rue des Tovets, 73120   +33 (0)4 79 08 12 74

HOTELS

Hotel Les Airelles

A tyrolean style hotel with breathtaking natural beauty and a rustic appearance set in the most beautiful part of Courchevel. If you dine on the terrace you are given warm slippers and hot wine. An ice rink on the front terrace runs from the start of the season until mid January.
Le Jardin Alpin, 73120
+33 (0)4 79 00 38 38   www.airelles.fr

Cheval Blanc

The new luxury hotel owned by Bernard Arnault. An eye-catching interior, the hotel comprises of suites and two penthouses. On a quiet and Alpine setting on the Jardin Alpin. Also has a very good restaurant.
Le Jardin Alpin, 73120
+33 (0)4 79 00 50 50   www.chevalblanc.com

Les Suites de la Potinière

The former La Potinière hotel reopened in 2009 as a deluxe complex of 15 suites, an apartment block, lounge bar and spa. Located in the heart of 1850.
Rue du Plantret, 73120
+33 (0)4 79 08 00 16   www.suites-potiniere.com

Le Mélézin

An Aman resorts property with large rooms and bathrooms designed with the skier in mind. A salon with open fire, cocktail bar and fumoir lounge. A Capri

stone indoor swimming pool and two Jacuzzis. Ideally located beside the Bellecote slope with ski-in ski-out. One of the best, however their restaurant is not as good as Cheval Blanc.

Rue de Bellecôte, 73120   +33 (0)4 79 08 01 33

Le Saint Roch

A new boutique 4-star hotel in Courchevel 1850 with 5 luxury contemporary rooms, 14 suites with hammam and a private apartment. With Carita spa, pool, ski-in ski-out and intimate lounge and piano bar.

Piste de Bellecôte, BP3, 73121
+33 (0)4 79 08 02 66   www.lesaintroch.com

Hotel la Sivolière

A chalet-style hotel situated in the woods just above the centre of Courchevel. Typical Savoyard style with wood carvings and fire places but with a modern edge. Ski-in ski-out and with its own ski shop, pool, Jacuzzi and massage services, everything you need is in one place.

Rue des Chenus, 73120
+33 (0)4 79 08 08 33   www.hotel-la-sivoliere.com

THINGS TO DO

As a popular winter destination Courchevel has a vast number of winter activities on offer and offer more outdoor activities than you can possibly do in one trip.

Air Tours

With Aéro-Club des Trois Vallées, experience the beauty of the French Alps from above with these fantastic air tours.

+33 (0)4 79 00 20 64   www.aeroclub3vallees.com

Buggy Kart Cross

It may be less graceful than skis but speeding through the winter snow at the purpose built Activ+ circuit guarantees some noisy fun.

+ 33 (0)6 65 57 17 29   Eric.courchevel@free.fr

Chemins du Baroque

Learn more about the regions baroque architecture with these guided tours of the local churches.

+33 (0)4 79 60 59 00   www.savoie-patrimoine.com

Cookery Courses

Whatever your level of skill, Michel Rochedy can help you hone your skills to impress your friends.

+33 (0)4 79 08 00 55   www.chabichou-courchevel.com

SPAS AND RELAXATION

Even if you are not staying at the hotel Byblos try out their Spa-Hammam.

Le Jardin Alpin, 73120   +33 (0)4 79 00 98 00

TRAVEL

Courchevel's central location means it has excellent airport coverage and is only two hours away from Geneva, Lyon and Grenoble international airports.

TAXIS

Courchevel Prestige Taxis

With flat rates to all three airports, Courchevel Prestige provides a friendly service that takes the pain out of transfers.

+33 (0)6 09 40 19 10   www.courchevel-prestige.com

SAF-Air Courchevel Helicopter Taxi

Forget the traffic jams and make transfers an event, SAF provides more than just transfers offering a variety of flights and bespoke services.

+33 (0)4 79 08 00 91   www.air-courchevel.com

USEFUL CONTACTS

Courchevel Tourist Board
+33 (0)4 79 08 00 29
www.courchevel.com

Société des Trois Vallées
www.s3v.com
The Société can provide information on weather
reports, ski passes and ski lifts.

EMERGENCY NUMBERS
Courchevel 1850
Medical Centres
Chalet Lafrage   +33 (0)4 79 08 48 54

Le Forum   +33 (0)4 79 08 32 13

Courchevel 1650
Maalej Adnene   +33 (0)4 79 08 04 45

Le Praz
Pierre Noblins   +33 (0)4 79 08 43 24

LA GRAVE

The charming 12th century village of La Grave, the spectacular mountain, La Meije and the skiing on the Dôme de la Lauze make up one of the most unusual ski resorts in the world.

La Grave offers 2,150 m vertical of relentless, uncompromising, high Alpine skiing – one of the longest vertical drops in the world, full of every hazard known to skiers. This is a virtual obstacle course from top to bottom.

The winter season runs from mid-December through until early May.

SURROUNDINGS

La Grave's alluring fresh powder is like the forbidden treasure in an Indiana Jones film, but the treasure is surrounded by perilous seracs, crevasses, cliffs, precipices, steep, avalanche-prone couloirs and concealed logs, rocks and tree stumps. For skiers looking for a challenge, La Grave offers it in spades.

La Grave can be as good as it gets for off-piste skiers, but the total lack of pistes makes it a very bad place to be if there has not been any fresh snow for a while and the mountain is icy or wind-packed. At times like that, it is best to ski in the more conventional resorts of Les Deux Alpes, Alpe d'Huez, or Serre Chevalier – all within an hour by car.

Girose de Droite

A long spectacular run from the Dôme da la Lauze, beginning on the glacier, continuing through high altitude bowls and couloirs, ending in the forest.

Tree Skiing

Between P2 (2,400 m) and P1 (1,800 m) is some of the best tree skiing in the world. Set among widely spaced larch trees, there are endless routes and paths between the trees. This is the only possible place to ski when the weather is bad in La Grave.

Etc.

There are many more classic routes in La Grave including Vallon de la Meije, Couloir Rama, Col de la Lauze to name but a few. Most of these are extreme routes involving rappelling and no-fall zones. Even if you are an expert skier, detailed discussion with your guide is essential before deciding which routes you feel willing and able to attempt.

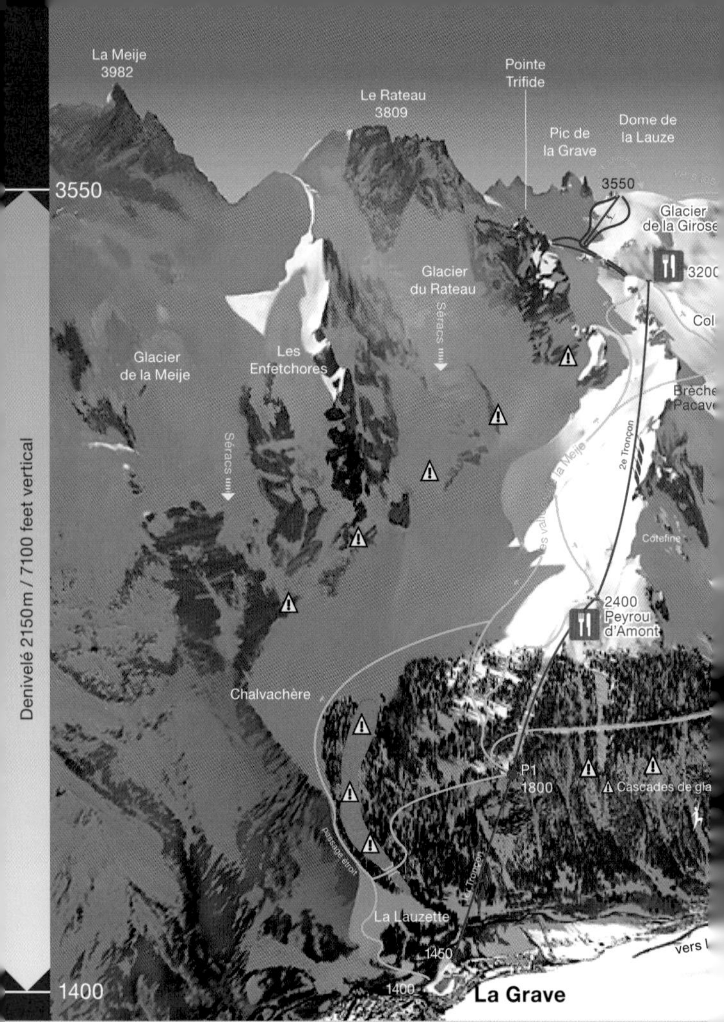

La Meije
3982

Le Rateau
3809

Pointe
Trifide

Pic de
la Grave

Dome de
la Lauze

3550

Glacier
de la Girose

3200

Col

Glacier
du Rateau

Bréche
Pacave

Glacier
de la Meije

Les
Enfetchores

Séracs

Côtefine

Séracs

2400
Peyrou
d'Amont

Chalvachère

P1
1800

Cascades de gla

La Lauzette

1450

1400

La Grave

3550

Denivelé 2150m / 7100 feet vertical

1400

MOUNTAINS

MOUNTAIN GUIDES

Guiding is essential virtually everywhere in La Grave. This is not a resort to follow someone else's ski tracks. Many routes require glacial harnesses and ropes for mandatory rappels and La Grave attracts the kind of skiers who ski with these items as standard equipment.

Philippe André
Has been a mountain guide for over 25 years and is one of the best in the area for off-piste, freeriding and heli-skiing.
+33 (0)6 80 22 84 75   racinesurf@aol.com

Skiers Lodge Guide Service

An international group of ski guides headed by Swedish mountain guide Pelle Lang who set up in La Grave in 1989. They love these mountains and enjoy nothing more than to share their enthusiasm and experience with newcomers to La Grave.

+33 (0)4 76 11 03 18   www.skierslodge.com

EQUIPMENT

Original La Grave

A local organiser of events as well as retail, Original is the centre of the freeriding set in La Grave.

91, place du Téléphérique, 05320   +33 (0)4 76 79 11 70

RESTAURANTS

RESTAURANTS IN TOWN

Hotel Le Sérac
Traditional French meals and a good international wine list. A large south facing balcony provides for magnificent views of La Meije.
Hotel-Restaurant «Le Sérac», 05320   +33 (0)4 76 79 91 53

La Plage du Macoomba
Always busy and open until midnight often with live music.
La Plage du Macoomba, 05320   +33 (0)4 76 79 80 69

Auberge Edelweiss
Has a gourmet French restaurant serving 4 course mountain specialities as well as fondue and raclette. A large selection of French wines carefully selected by the owner.
Auberge Edelweiss, 05320   +33 (0)4 76 79 90 93

Au Vieux Guide
An excellent restaurant in La Meije with quality traditional food and a cosy atmosphere.
Le Village, 05320   +33 (0)4 76 79 90 75

APRÈS-SKI

La Grave does not offer much in the way of après-ski, which is quite alright, since after a full day of putting your life on the line, you may welcome a nap as the perfect after-ski activity anyway. If you have energy left, you can swap tall tales about cliff jumping and avalanche surfing with grizzled veterans of the world's off-piste circuit in any one of a handful of local restaurants.

Auberge Edelweiss
Has a friendly bar which is a good spot for a nightcap or aperitif.
Auberge Edelweiss, 05320   +33 (0)4 76 79 90 93

Pub Le Bois des Fées
This place always attracts the crowds and has the occasional live band.
+33 (0)4 76 11 05 48

HOTELS

Skiers Lodge/Hotel des Alpes

A cosy accommodation where you will feel at home, this hotel's history goes back to 1898 and it is situated just a five minute walk from the lift.

Attracts some of the best skiers in the world through the ski school. The views from the terrace and sauna across the valley are breathtaking.

Skiers Lodge, 05320

+33 (0)4 76 11 03 18 www.lodge.la-grave.com

Les Chalets de la Meije

Is centrally located and has a true French village feel. Choose from hotel, chalet or apartments for a quiet and comfortable stay.

Le nouveau village, 05320

+33 (0)4 76 79 97 97 www.chalet-meije.com

Auberge Edelweiss

Has simple and basic rooms. They also have a Black Diamond test ski centre. Good restaurant and bar.

Auberge Edelweiss, 05320

+33 (0)4 76 79 90 93 www.hotel-edelweiss.com

THINGS TO DO

La Grave's status as a relatively small resort has allowed much of its cultural heritage to remain intact and can boast many churches and buildings that have weathered the centuries to this day.

Paragliding

Enjoy La Grave's wondrous landscape from above with the professionals from Air Vif.

+33 (0)4 76 79 21 05   www.aventurier.fr

Derby de la Meije

An annual event in early April to celebrate the fresh snow, this race sees serious competitors in high-tech gear matched against curious feather and fur-clad characters.

+33 (0)4 76 79 90 05   www.derbydelameije.com

TRAVEL

Most local travel links are between Grenoble airport and La Grave, if travelling from Lyon, phone your hotel or the Tourist Board for travel advice.

PUBLIC TRANSPORT
Coach
Regular coach service runs from Grenoble station to La Grave.
+33 (0)8 82 12 02 22 03

Taxi de la Meije
La Grave's local taxi service provides a shuttle service between La Grave and Grenbole. Book in advance.
+33 (0)6 79 53 45 67   www.taxidelameije.com

Megève ● ● Chamonix
Les Contamines ●

Lyon   ● Courmayeur

Val d'Isère/Tignes

Courchevel ●   ●

USEFUL CONTACTS

La Grave Tourist Board
+33 (0)4 76 79 90 05
www.lagrave-lameije.com

Mountain Guide Office
+33 (0)4 76 79 90 21
www.guidelagrave.com

Lift Operator   +33 (0)4 76 79 91 09

Snow and Avalanche Bulletins   +33 (0)8 92 68 10 20

EMERGENCY NUMBERS
Mountain Rescue   +33 (0)8 92 68 10

Doctor   +33 (0)4 76 79 79 98 03

VAL D'ISÈRE

This ski area (1,850 m), which the legendary French ski hero Jean-Claude Killy calls home, is the ultimate in versatility. Close to 140 trails of free-skiing terrain exceeds the groomed runs by far. Narrow couloirs, steep bowls, winding canyons, glacial terrain and even some tree-skiing can be found in this resort that really has it all.

Over the last decade Val d'Isère has lost its innocence. It has become big business, grown and moved upmarket, however, it still retains a lot of charm and as Alain Ledoux says, «Val d'Isère offers all that Chamonix does but without the risks».
Having said that, it is also where Jorn Werdelin skied off a cliff and broke his back in 1996 and thereby, in part, gave birth to the idea of Linde Werdelin.

The winter season runs from late November to early May.

SURROUNDINGS

There are a few couloirs of note here, but the emphasis is on a different type of terrain with a combination of moguls, open off-piste skiing and a bit of tree-skiing as well.

The list of interesting runs and off-piste routes are too numerous to mention, but here are a few to get you started.

Solaise (2,560 m)

The black piste is a long bump run - heaven or hell depending how much you like bumps. Either way, if your legs don't get lactic acid overdose on this run you must have a red and yellow "S" on your chest. There are also off-piste variations from Solaise

on Danaïdes and Le Lavancher couloir that take skiers into the trees and ultimately end up in either Le Laisinant or Le Fornet.

Arcelle

From the top of the Manchet Express lift, there are many off-piste variations of the Arcelle Piste. These are not that steep and are excellent fare in corn snow conditions.

Tour de Charvet

This is not so difficult and very picturesque. It is a good way of getting from Tignes across to the upper slopes of Val d'Isère without skiing all the way down to

town. The route begins at the Grand Pre lift taking you across to the Manchet Express, before a final decent via the Solaise.

Vallée Perdue (The Lost Valley)

You reach this hidden piste from the La Daille cable car, but it is no easy find – hence its name. You ski this run as a sightseeing experience rather than for the skiing itself but it is definitely worth the trouble. It is an undulating, narrow canyon that winds its way around all kinds of obstacles including sections of natural tunnel.

Couloir des Pisteurs

A twenty-minute hike from the top of the Grand Pre lift, this is one of the best couloirs in Val d'Isère. It's not only a thrilling technical run at the top, but also gives the only access to some good open slopes lower down. The entry is often icy and falling is not an option, so it might be good to have some rope handy.

North Face of the Pointe Pers

This is perhaps our favourite descent in Val d'Isère. It begins with a hike from the top of the Aiguille Pers Montets lift. The entry can be very difficult making a guide helpful. The run begins with a beautiful, wide steep pitch and then meanders around the mountain, ending up winding through the picturesque Gorges de Malpasset until you ultimately reach Le Fornet.

MOUNTAINS

MOUNTAIN GUIDES
Alain Ledoux
An experienced guide and ski instructor at Mountain Masters Ski School at Killy Sport. Even in thick fog he can negotiate you down to town.

+33 (0)6 80 07 67 04   www.mountain-masters.com

EQUIPMENT
Decales
Killy Sports luxury boutique stocking brands such as Prada, Paul and Joe and Marc Jacob.

Val Village, 73150   +33 (0)4 79 06 16 83

Surefoot
A modern clinic for your feet/boots. They make your feet feel like they are directly connected to the edge of your skis. They also have shops in Courchevel, Verbier and London to name a few.

Immeuble le Dome, 73150   +33 (0)4 79 09 76 60

RESTAURANTS

MOUNTAIN RESTAURANTS

L'Arbina
Just across the Aeroski telecabin in Le Lac. The best lunch you will find, including fantastic fish. Great food, service and a sunny terrace.

Le Rosset, Lac de Tignes, 73320 Tignes   +33 (0)4 79 06 34 78

La Fruitière
At the mid station of La Daille serving typical Savoyard food and wine. Sample the local cheeses.

Bellevarde Massif, 73150, La Daille   +33 (0)4 79 06 07 17

Les Marmottes
Enjoy the goulash soup by the fire in the heart of the Bellevarde ski area.

+33 (0)4 79 06 05 08

Edelweiss
On the run down to the bottom of the cable car serves great food. The terrace has views towards Bellevarde. Reservations essential.

Piste Mangard, Le Fornet, 73150   +33 (0)6 10 28 70 64

Le Signal
Is located at the top of the cable car in Le Fornet, the interior is very modern, with a nice little bar and not at all mountain like. The food is very good and there is a long dessert list.

Le Signal, 73150, Le Fornet, 73150   +33 (0)4 79 06 03 38

L'Arolay

Recommended for its table-top charcoal grilled braserades.

+33 (0)4 79 06 11 68   www.arolay.com

La Vieille Maison

Once an old farmhouse in La Daille it now serves hearty Savoyard dishes in a cosy old-fashioned setting.

La Vieille Maison, 73150, La Daille   +33 (0)4 79 06 11 76

Les Clochetons

Traditional French food in a delightful and authentic ambience and offers a free limousine service.

Vallée du Manchet, 73150   +33 (0)4 79 41 13 11

HOTELS

Hotel Les Barmes de L'Ours

The best hotel in Val d'Isère at the foot of the Bellevarde Olympic ski run with ski-in ski-out.
Exclusive facilities including three restaurants and a Michelin star, and one of the largest and best spas in the Alps. The top suites have their own fireplace and jacuzzi. It has a beautiful ambience and exceptional service. Chemin des Carats, 73150
+33 (0)4 79 41 37 00   www.hotel-les-barmes.com

Hotel Christiania

Ideally located in the centre of the resort and close to the ski lift. Family run and recently refurbished with an excellent restaurant overlooking the slopes.
Hotel Christiana, BP 48, 73152
+33 (0)4 79 06 08 25   www.hotel-christiania.com

Hotel Le Blizzard

Has charming rooms, a good restaurant and heated outdoor swimming pool. Le Blizzard, BP 64, 73150
+33 (0)4 79 06 02 07   www.hotelblizzard.com

Le Savoie

After opening last year, has now been upgraded to a 4-star luxury hotel (France doesn't have 5-star ratings). Relax in the spa. Ski room with Pro Shop Killy Sport. Also has a good French restaurant with south-facing terrace and cocktail bar. Avenue Olympique, 73150
+33 (0)4 79 00 01 15   www.lesavoie.com

THINGS TO DO

Val d'Isère is packed with non-ski activities that will get your adrenaline pumping. Try paragliding, ice climbing, ice driving, snowshoe randonnées, air boarding or husky sleighs on Le Lac.

The town also plays host to a variety of festivals and events throughout the winter months; kicking off with the 'First Tracks' opening weekend on the last weekend of November and carrying on through to April and ranging from the Polo Masters Cup to the Adventure and Discovery Film Festival, Val d'Isère hosts a huge variety of winter events to keep visitors entertained.

For a more sedate pace, the local tourist office also provides a wealth of activities and should be your first stop if you are seeking something more relaxed.

Igloo evenings

Spend an unforgettable evening at 2,400 m in a genuine igloo village. Get there by helicopter or snow scooter, enjoy a meal and descend by torchlight.
+33 (0)6 15 19 46 29   www.alaska-motoneige.com

Village Discovery

With tours in both French and English organised by the tourist office, get to know the personality and history of Val d'Isère. Every Tuesday (Monday in April); 10:00 am in French, 11:30 am in English.
+33 (0) 79 06 06 60

La ferme de L'Adroit

Visit Xavier for a guided tour of his farm and a chance to taste some locally produced cheese. The farm is located on a small road that turns off from the road leading to Le Fornet.

+33 (0)4 79 06 13 02   www.fermedeladroit.com

French Patisserie Classes

"Best French Pastrycook award", offering classes in a variety of baking techniques, followed by a tasting session.

+33 (0)4 79 06 16 09

Discover Local Crafts in Seez

Guided tours (in French) of local craft industries including: spinning, taxidermy, gold/silversmith, blacksmith, tannery and local craft centre.
+33 (0)4 79 41 00 15

«Critérium de la Première Neige»

Part of the 2009 'Alpine Skiing World Cup Events', this promises to be an exciting two weeks in mid-December of world-class racing.
+33 (0)4 79 06 03 49

SPAS AND RELAXATION

With eight spas located throughout Val d'Isère there is a huge choice if you feel the need for a little pampering and recuperation after a hard day on the slopes.
The Les Barmes de l'Ours and Blizzard Hotel are to be particularly recommended for their luxurious modern facilities.

Les Barmes de L'Ours
Chemin des Carats, 73150   +33 (0)4 79 41 37 00

Hotel Blizzard
Le Blizzard, BP 64, 73150   +33 (0)4 79 06 02 07

Hotel Christiania
The spa facilities at the Hotel Christiania are second to none, with an extensive range of services ranging from shiatsu all the way through to cosmetic treatments.
Hotel Christiana, BP 48, 73150   +33 (0)4 79 06 08 25

Sion

Geneva

Verbier

Chamonix

Megève

Les Contamines

Courmayeu

Lyon

Val d'Isère/Tignes

Courchevel

Grenoble

La Grave

Sestrie

TRAVEL

Geneva, Lyon, Chambéry and Grenoble airports serve Val d'Isère, with shuttle services running to all four.

PUBLIC TRANSPORT
Altibus
Altibus provides a realiable service to Geneva, Lyon and Chambéry.
+33 (0)4 79 68 32 96   www.altibus.com

Autocar Monet
If arriving from Grenoble then Monet is the coach company for you.
+33 (0)4 76 93 40 00

TAXIS AND PRIVATE HIRE
Taxis Bozzetto
With a long history in the area Bozzetto provides both taxis and private hire cars.
+33 (0)6 03 75 03 75   www.taxis-bozzetto.com

USEFUL CONTACTS

Tourist Office
   +33 (0)4 79 06 06 60
   info@valdisere.com   www.valdisere.com

Ski Patrol
   +33 (0)4 79 06 02 10
   Service.pistes@valdisere.fr

EMERGENCY NUMBERS

Cabinet Médical du Centre	+33 (0)4 79 06 06 11
Cabinet Médical du Val Village	+33 (0)4 79 06 13 70
Cabinet Médical Médival	+33 (0)4 79 40 26 80

TIGNES

The nature of the skiing in Tignes is somewhat different than in Val d'Isère. Tignes is divided into the general areas of Palet/L'Aiguille Percée, La Grande Motte, Tovière and Les Brévières. If you have the technical skills involved in negotiating turns in steep and narrow couloirs, you will reach Nirvana here. The list is almost endless.

Some of these couloirs are interesting only for the challenge, while others are a means to an end, giving access to long slopes of powder that can not be reached in any other way. Access to most of the chutes require a hike of anywhere from fifteen minutes to one hour.
They are all avalanche-prone directly after a snowfall, so a professional guide is recommended.

The winter season lasts from December to April, with April often seeing the freshest conditions as the spring showers fall as snow.

SURROUNDINGS

Couloirs du Chardonnet
   Although they are short, these are some of our
   favourite chutes in Tignes. They are easily accessible
   with a short hike from the top of the Grattalu Chair.
   North facing and wind protected, they generally have
   wonderful snow if you get there first.

The Grande Motte
   Reaching an altitude of 3,656 m, the Grande Motte
   Glacier is the highest skiing point in Tignes.

   There are a couple of interesting off-piste routes here—a
   south-facing couloir down the back side which is
   quite straightforward and the North face of the glacier,

which requires a guide to lead skiers amidst the seracs and crevasses. The funicular from Val Claret will get you most of the way there, hop on the Grand Motte cable-car to reach the very top.

Dôme de Pramecou

If you are very bold, you can ski across the flat part of the glacier and hike the Pramecou to descend the north face. The entry is treacherous – close to 50 degrees with rocks below.

After a few turns above the rocks, you can ski out to your left, where it is still steep, but the clear path of snow down to the flats allows the lump in your throat to subside.

Tour de la Grande Balme

Setting off from the top of the Grande Motte cable car, this is a delightful route, not as dangerous as the Grande Balme couloirs or the Pramecou, which begins with some skiing and hiking in the valley between the two peaks.

Ultimately, it reaches some excellent off-piste terrain that ends up on the north face below the Grande Balme's chutes; better to do this before mid February when the Te, TeleT el, Telesiege des Ves opens up and gives easier access to this back side; after this time it might not be worth the walk!

Tufs Couloirs

Positioned between the trolles and piste H on Toviere, these are very narrow chutes in places and no hike is required to get to them. However, there is a certain difficulty in access–finding your way into the correct gully! Easy to see and scout from Tignes 2,100 there might be a great couloir and an unskiable one side by side. To try and figure out which one you are entering approaching from the opposite side is no easy task.

Vallon de la Sache

Tignes is not only a collection of couloirs–it does have more open terrain as well. A good example of a long lovely run with many variations that does not require constant focus is the Vallon de la Sache. Beginning near the famous rock formation, Aiguille Percée (Eye of the Needle), this run takes you all the way down to Tignes les Brevières, a nice spot to have lunch, with various restaurants to choose from in the old village.

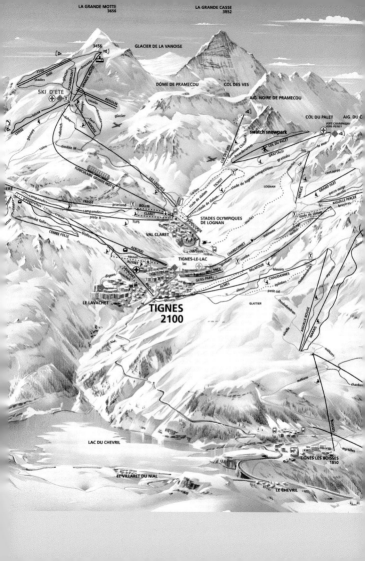

MOUNTAINS

MOUNTAIN GUIDES
Tetra Hors piste

Offering a variety of programme options, including heli-ski, these experienced guides will help you make the most of the off-piste opportunities.

+33 (0)6 31 49 92 75 www.tetrahp.com

Evolution 2

Whether you are a seasoned pro or just making those first tentative steps, Evolution 2 can cater for all skill ranges and offers a huge range of winter sports to get into.

+33 (0)4 79 06 43 78 www.evolution2.com

EQUIPMENT
Helly Hansen

A large store with a huge range of equipment and expert staff on hand to answer any questions you may have.

Neige et soleil, 73320, Tignes le Lac +33 (0)4 79 06 46 93

RESTAURANTS

MOUNTAIN RESTAURANTS
La Tovière
With beautiful panoramic views from the peak of the mountain and delicious homemade waffles; La Tovière will soon be celebrating its 40th anniversary.

+33 (0)4 79 06 35 05 www.restaurant-tignes2700.com

Le Panoramic
Located at the foot of the Grande Motte glacier, Le Panoramic offers good food in a warm and relaxing atmosphere.

+33 (0)4 79 06 47 21

RESTAURANTS IN TOWN
Le Hors Piste
Offering a variety of local specialities, bistro food and a gourmet menu, the restaurant Le Hors Piste is worth a visit even if you are not staying at the hotel Le Ski d'Or.

Hotel Ski D'Or, 73320, Tignes Val Claret +33 (0)4 79 06 51 60

Auberge des 3 Oursons
With its rustic interior the restaurant is the perfect setting for their traditional Savoyard cooking.

Les Neiges D'Or, 73320, Tignes Val Claret
+33 (0)4 79 06 35 66

APRÈS SKI

Whitney Bar

A relaxed bar with luxurious style and fantastic drinks;
worth a visit for their idiosyncratic fireplace alone.
Le Whitney Bar dans «Les Suites du Nevada»,
73330, Tignes Val Claret   +33 (0)4 79 01 11 43

THINGS TO DO

*There is a wealth of opportunities to use up any last
reserves of energy in Tignes, from ice climbing to
snow-mobiles and helicopter tours, there are dozens of
possibilities.*
*Contact the Tourist Board for opportunities and prices
(see Useful Contacts).*

Ice Diving

Plunge into the icy depths of the frozen Lake Tignes
and explore the eerie mysteries beneath the ice.
+33 (0)4 79 06 43 78   www.evolution2.com

The «Heart of Tignes» heritage centre

Witness seven centuries of local history at this
interactive museum; admission is free.
+33 (0)4 79 40 04 40

TRAVEL

Tignes' closest air link is Chambery, followed by Lyon and Geneva, all three are serviced by good public transport services (see map page 154).

TAXIS AND PRIVATE HIRE

A&A Taxi

+33 (0)6 09 51 90 99   www.taxitignes.fr

A.A. Anémone Mont-Jovet Cédric

+33 (0)6 09 41 01 46   www.anemone-taxi.com

USEFUL CONTACTS

Tignes Information
 +33 (0)4 79 40 04 40
 www.tignes.net

Lift Operators
 +33 (0)4 79 06 60 12
 stgm@compagniedesalpes.fr

Piste Security
 +33 (0)4 79 06 32 00   pistes@tignes.net

EMERGENCY NUMBERS
Medical Centres
 Le Lac   +33 (0)4 79 06 50 07

 Le Val Claret   +33 (0)4 79 06 59 64

 Ambulance Anita Desvallon   +33 (0)4 79 06 59 18

NATIONAL EMERGENCY NUMBERS

European Emergency Phone Number   112

SAMU - Emergency services   15

Gendarmerie - Police and mountain rescue   17

Brigade - Accident, fire and mountain rescue   18

Whilst we would love to spend every day
of the season skiing in each resort,
we just don't have the time!

Therefore we welcome any comments,
suggestions or feedback from you.

Please email skiguide@lindewerdelin.com

— • —

Credits

O.T. Chamonix Mont-Blanc - Courchevel Tourisme
O.T. des Contamines-Montjoie - O.T. Megève
Tignes Développement - O.T. Val d'Isère - Auberge Edelweiss
Hotel Albert 1er - Aman Resorts/Hotel Le Mélézin
Hotel Christiana - Flocons de Sel - Idéal 1850
L'Ô à la bouche - La Compagnie du Mont-Blanc - Les Airelles
Les Barmes de l'Ours - Les Enfants Terribles - La Ferme
Les Fermes de Marie - La Folie Douce - La Fruitière
La Grande Ourse - Pier Paul Jack - Les Suites de la Potinière
Quartz Bar - Agence 14 Septembre - J.-C. Amiel - E. Bargis
E. Bergoend - S. Berthe - Bionnassayimages.com - B. Boone
M. Colonel - M. Dalmasso - D. Derisbourg - L. Di Orio
Eclipse - E. Giroud - J. Hadik - T. Hjarnoe/Tuala.com
C. Jaccoux/Black Crows - J. Kélagopian - T. Lamiche
P. Leroy/Semaphore - C. Margot - F. Moscatello- Nuts
P. Pachod - J. Pontin - L. Reversade - E. Saillet - Ph. Schaff
N. Tosi - P. Vallet - H. Zeegers

Illustrations Dominique Bertail / module-etrange.com

Beautiful Books

First published 2009

Beautiful Books Limited
36-38 Glasshouse Street
London W1B 5DL

www.beautiful-books.co.uk

ISBN 9781905636747

Copyright © Morten Linde and Jorn Werdelin 2009

— • —

A catalogue reference for this book
is available from the British Library

— • —